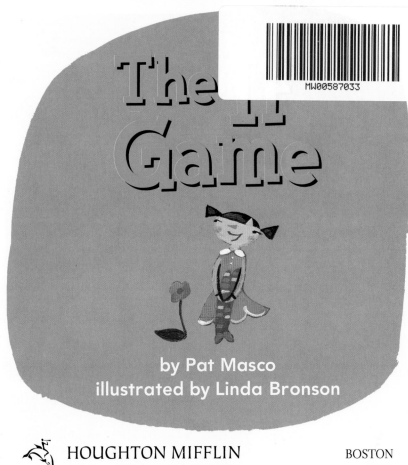

The Ii Game

by Pat Masco
illustrated by Linda Bronson

HOUGHTON MIFFLIN   BOSTON

Printed in China

ISBN 10: 0-618-88623-0
ISBN 13: 978-0-618-88623-4

17 18 19 20 21 0940 21 20 19 18 17
4500648149

Ned and Pam were best friends.
Every day, after school, they would play.
Sometimes they played Simon Says.
Other times, they played the If game.

"If 740 meteors are falling from the sky," said Pam. "And 90 more begin to fall. How many are falling?"

"Watch out!" said Ned. "Run for cover!"

Read • Think • Write   What is 740 plus 90 ?

"If 600 rhinos are charging," said Pam.

"And 200 more start to run.

How many rhinos are charging?"

"Watch out!" said Ned. "Run for cover!"

Read • Think • Write What is 600 plus 200?

"If 435 pounds of snow is sliding down a mountain," said Pam.

"Then 109 more pounds begin to slide. How many pounds slide in all?"

"Watch out!" said Ned. "Run for cover!"

Read • Think • Write   What is 435 plus 109?

5

"If 580 bees are swarming," said Pam.
"And 372 bees join them.
How many bees are swarming?"
"Watch out!" said Ned. "Run—"

Read • Think • Write   What is 580 plus 372?

6

"You might take this game more seriously,"
interrupted Pam.

"Why?" asked Ned.

"Because here they come!" said Pam.

"Run!" said Ned.

Rhino Run, Rhino Drink

Show

Follow Directions, Oral and Written

Show 400 rhinos running and 200 rhinos drinking at a pond.

Share

Talk about how to subtract 200 from 600.

Write

Write a number sentence to show 200 rhinos leaving a group of 600 rhinos.